How & Why Birds Build N

Birds build nests to make homes for their young. They build many kinds of nests, in many different places.

This yellow warbler is building a nest in a tree. Here her babies will be safe from cats and other animals that might want to eat them. The warbler weaves together soft, silky plant fibers to make her nest.

The hummingbird is tiny, and so is its nest. A female hummingbird makes her nest from mosses, spiderwebs, and plants called lichens.

The nest is a soft cradle for her eggs. This picture shows a single egg, which is no bigger than a pea! The hummingbird sits on the eggs to keep them warm until they hatch.

Flickers nest inside dead trees. They use their beaks to peck away the soft, rotting wood and make a hollow in the trunk. When their eggs hatch, the parent birds bring food to the babies.

The young birds stay safe inside the tree until they grow feathers and are big enough to fly. This youngster is almost ready to leave the nest.

A barn swallow nest is tucked high in the beams of an old barn. The swallows shape their nests from mud, which hardens as it dries.

Once the eggs hatch, the parent swallows are busy all day. They catch insects and bring the insects to the nest to feed their young. Young birds are always hungry!

Like many birds that live on seacoasts, terns nest on the ground. An arctic tern has gathered bits of grass to make a place for her eggs among the rocks. The speckled eggs look like little stones.

So do the fluffy babies that hatch from them! Their coloring helps them stay hidden.

Atlantic puffins are ocean birds that nest on rocky coasts. This puffin has found a good place for its nest.

The puffin has dug a hole, or burrow, under a rock. The burrow is lined with grass. The female puffin lays only one egg. Inside the burrow, the puffin and her egg are safe and warm.

Kingfishers nest in sandy banks along streams. The parents tunnel into the bank, using their beaks and feet to dig. The female lays her eggs at the end of the tunnel.

Young kingfishers are naked and blind when they hatch. When they grow feathers, they look like little adults. Soon they will be ready to leave the nest and go off on their own.

Use the information in this book to answer some "how and why" questions.

- Why does the yellow warbler build its nest in a tree?

- Why does a hummingbird sit on her eggs?

- Why are barn swallow parents busy all day?

- How do terns make nests on the ground?

- How does the puffin line its burrow?

- How do kingfishers dig their nesting tunnels?